Reinventing New Chapters in Your Life at Any Age

7 Steps to Making It Happen

Nadia Giordana

Reinventing New Chapters in Your Life at Any Age

7 Steps to Making It Happen

Nadia Giordana

Published by Cloud 9 Publishing

ISBN 10: 1-886352-38-0
ISBN 13: 978-1-886352-38-4

ACKNOWLEDGMENTS

I am deeply grateful to Connie Anderson of WordsAndDeedsInc.com for her editorial assistance and suggestions. She is unfailingly accurate and unflappable. I can depend on her. Thanks must also go to Laura Breider Behrendt, who lent her technical expertise in a dozen different ways. Contributing authors, Sid Korpi, Kathi Holmes, and Barb Greenberg, three lovely ladies who shared their personal stories were especially important to this project. Without them, there would have been a missing element. Their individual accounts, though vastly different, each mirrors the principles in this book. And a second thank you from my heart, to Sid Korpi (Proof Positive Editing) for taking the time to give this book a final once-over.

Author's websites and social media access:

EmbodyYourVision.com
ThinkingSkinny.com
WomanVision.tv
NadiaGiordana.com
Twitter: @NadiaGiordana
linkedin.com/in/nadiagiordana

Facebook.com/nadia.giordana.media

DEDICATION

To Norman and Sylvia Wilkins, two of the most creative, adaptable, and adventuresome people I've ever known. They lived their lives fully and personified the principles outlined in this book.

TABLE OF CONTENTS

INTRODUCTION: What you need to know before you get started

Hi, I'm Nadia Giordana, an author, speaker, mentor, and lifestyle strategist. I help women in midlife find the inspiration they need to reactivate their sidelined personal life goals. I do this by helping each woman design roadmaps she can use to affect her personal transformation or create new chapters in her life.

Think about this quote by Edwin Lewis Cole:

You don't drown by falling in the water; you drown by staying there.

A few years ago, I experienced a devastating layoff, due to corporate downsizing. I was at an age when, if I had accepted the status quo, I would have simply retired and spent my time lunching with friends, babysitting grandchildren, and perfecting my golf swing. At first, I slipped right into that mindset. It would have been easy to choose to stay right there in that stage of life for the next decade or two. The pastimes I mentioned are all wonderful things (especially the part about grandchildren), but I couldn't help thinking to myself, *Is this all there is, now that I've reached a certain age*? *No!* Then came the "aha" moment, followed by the idea that I still have time to make my "second act" equally as exciting and fulfilling as my early years, and that I do have a choice in the matter. I realized my life isn't even close to being over—and *neither* is yours!

I decided to do something different with this chapter in my life. It was the making of this choice, in that moment, that changed my future.

Before I could begin, I needed to take a hard look at where I was in life at that moment. After that, I proceeded to figure out how and where I had slipped off track. Then I determined what was missing, where I wanted to be, and how I was going to get there. This all may sound simple enough, and in many ways it was, but it involved a lot of thought and planning.

First I worked on my personal transformation. For me, that meant losing weight—88 pounds to be exact, which I did in a relatively short period of time using healthy lifestyle changes, and without fad dieting or resorting to surgery.

Back in the 1970s as a young, 20-something woman, when it was considered offbeat to be eating whole foods and exercising, I became

what was then called a "health nut."
Embracing that lifestyle worked for me.

But even with the early imprinting about
healthy choices, the stresses of making my
way through the tangled and competitive
corporate world got the best of me. In my
mid-40s and into my 50s, the weight piled
on.

This went on for about 15 years, so it was not
like trying to lose baby weight. I was older;
my body was used to the extra weight, and it
didn't want to change.

At age 58, in 2006, I was laid off, as I
mentioned earlier. My life was turned upside
down, as I had planned to retire while
working there. Did being older and
overweight hasten my demise? Whatever the
reason, I spent a year nursing my wounded
pride, feeling old and useless, and wondering
if I should retire completely. Eventually, I got
over myself, and I decided I had a lot more
living to do. When I set about losing the
weight, I didn't want to go on a structured
diet. I knew that wouldn't work for me.

My entire lifestyle, and manner of thinking about food, had to change.

13

I remembered what I had learned about healthy eating in years past, researched new information, studied several popular diets for the best of what they had to offer, and began a methodical changeover in my lifestyle. One by one, I started replacing my bad habits with good ones.

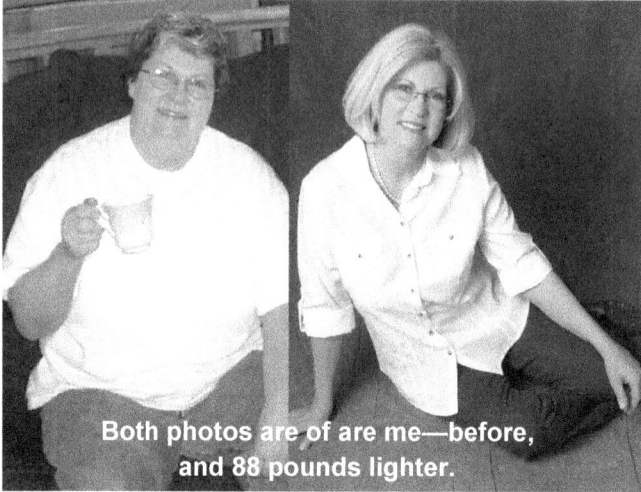

Both photos are of are me—before, and 88 pounds lighter.

I maintained a daily dialogue with God, and in that same mindset, I was keenly aware of the power of prayer, positive thinking, and visualization. Using these basic tools every day, I reached my first goal weight 10 months later without the benefit of exercise. In fact, I couldn't exercise because a leg injury (partially due to being overweight) prevented me from doing any weight-bearing exercise. But once I was 60 pounds lighter, the momentum continued, and over the following four months, I added exercise to my routine and reached my final weight goal. During this time period, I kept extensive notes and a food diary, thinking I might create a blog or write an article about my experiences. As time went on, I realized I had the makings of a book. Not long after reaching my weight goals, I set about writing and publishing *Thinking Skinny: Transform Any Healthy Weight-Loss Program into Supercharged Success*. My book was a 2010 finalist at the Midwest Independent Book Awards.

Today, I maintain my healthy lifestyle and attitude, and my weight is no longer an issue—at least not any more than normal maintenance, staying active, and paying attention to what I eat—that sort of thing.

I was so inspired by the weight loss, I decided to tackle another big stumbling block in my life—a deep-seated dread of public speaking. I proceeded to climb that mountain, too. I'll be honest with you about this one—I'm still at the first or second base camp, and I have a ways to go, but I'm making the climb. This will be an ongoing effort for me.

Working on my ability to speak in public to groups was a bigger challenge than losing weight, and I wasn't sure what to do first. I started with one or two very short speaking engagements, moving on to longer presentations. Then I began hosting an Internet radio show called "Interviews with Extraordinary Women." I was able to speak comfortably without becoming self-conscious. It helped that I placed my focus on my guests, and the spotlight wasn't directly on me.

Later, I got interested in video and used it to film my personal website introductions and several of my subsequent presentations. Adding a video camera to the mix of tools helped me even more with my speaking skills. You can begin to see how effective it was for me to do this in stages, and when we get to step #6, where I share my goal-setting techniques, you'll recognize them in some of the things I've just mentioned.

Overcoming these two huge hurdles (losing weight and overcoming my fear of speaking) made me feel younger, more alive, invincible, and unstoppable. How sad and full of regret would I have been if I had lived my entire life without conquering these things?

Remember—whatever your age, it's not too late to shake off negative self-talk and reinvent new chapters in your life.

Some might label me a coach, but that's not accurate. I'm not here to move you along your life path in the obvious sense. I'm a lifestyle strategist, and my job is to equip you with the tools to design a plan to fulfill desires you shelved years ago. This will allow you to remove *"I wish I had"* or take *"maybe someday"* out of your vocabulary. And you know what? When you accomplish something you've secretly always wanted to do, you become excited, happy, self-assured, and proud. That's when other aspects of your life begin to fall into place. You will be in a state of mind to address them with confidence. Because let's face it:

> ***Someday is here, and it's time for us to do the things we always said we were going to do.***

Focus: The Lifestyle GPS System™

I'm a lot like you. And like you, I have reinvented myself several times in my life— not always intentionally. Sometimes circumstances forced it on me. Only after someone pointed out that I had reinvented my life a number of times did I become consciously aware of what I was doing. From that moment, I began to do it with intent. I developed a customizable goal planning strategy (GPS) that quickly became the

Lifestyle GPS System™ that helps me write and create roadmaps for new adventures in my life. It includes my books, ebooks, workbook, DVDs and downloadable products—everything you need to design, plan, and execute your own personal transformation or start the next exciting new chapter in your life. For the latest updates, new products and information, go straight to my website at www.EmbodyYourVision.com. It's the direct link to the Lifestyle GPS System™ and its components.

I want to share it with you and teach you how I did it. Showing you how you can use what I've discovered will shorten the learning curve for you and help avoid some of the bumps, road-blocks, and detours you might run into.

I have a saying:

> *Lifestyle choices are a lot like buying new clothes. We try on different things until something fits, and even then, it doesn't fit forever, goes out of style, or we tire of it. It's up to us to discard a bad fit as soon as it's recognized.*

Let's get started. The meaning here is all-encompassing. Your reinvention may be personal (weight loss or relationships, for example), or perhaps spiritual (realigning with your God or your higher self), it could be social skills (public speaking or sales and marketing techniques). Maybe it's overcoming fears (you already know mine; what are some of yours?), or it may be that you've always wanted to start your own business.

It's okay if your plans change as you go along. Just get started. If it becomes apparent that your goals need to be revised, then do that. This is a fluid process. Also, it's not necessary that you go through the seven steps in any particular sequence—or even that, in your case, you need to do all seven. Start where you feel you will have the most immediate success, and work through the rest. You may find, for example, that your personal relationships are in good shape. Great! That means you are closer than you thought, so you can work on something else.

Is your dream new—or a lifelong one?

Let's stop here for a moment. I'm assuming you already have an idea of what this new chapter in your life is going to be. This is especially true if it is an old dream or a lifelong desire that you want to put into action. If not, and you're more at a point where you're feeling like you want something more in your life, but you aren't sure what

19

that "something more" looks like, take a step back, right now before moving on to the 7 steps. Theyt are designed to help implement your reinvention.

Take some time, a day or a weekend, away from TV and other distractions, and put some thought into what it is you want. It will come to you if you give it priority, and allow its image to find its way into your thoughts. You may be surprised to find that your dream was there all along, sitting quietly in the back seat of your consciousness, waiting for you to resurrect it. Okay. Do you have it? Good, then let's begin.

Now, before we go forward, realize that you must be willing to risk failure. We've all heard this concept before, but it is true: Each failure brings us one step closer to success. If you have a false start or two, stumble once or twice, so be it.

Balance it with the knowledge that you're narrowing the distance between you and the finish line.

REINVENTING NEW CHAPTERS IN YOUR LIFE AT ANY AGE:
7 Steps to Making It Happen

7 STEPS TO REINVENTING NEW CHAPTERS IN YOUR LIFE

1. **Reshaping** a healthier body and attitude:

   This is #1 for a good reason. It's the cornerstone of your success, and regardless of whether you have a lot of work to do in this area (like I did), or you think you are in pretty good shape, having a healthier body will give you the foundation and physical energy to pursue your dreams. Without it, you won't have the stamina to reach your "showstopper" goal. More about this at step #6).

   You can get healthier, physically and emotionally, in a number of ways, and that's naturally going to be different for each of you. I'm certainly not an expert. But— if your issue is weight, you might be interested in my book, *Thinking Skinny.* It's available at

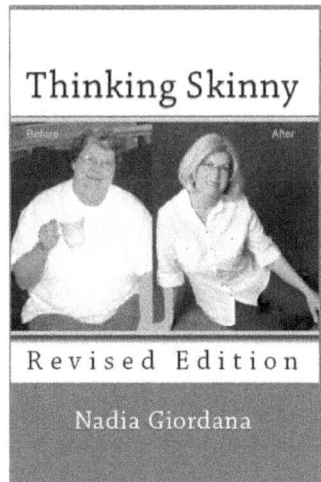

ThinkingSkinny.com and also nationwide at Amazon.com. Here you can learn details about my own weight loss journey.

No matter who you are, and where you are with regard to fitness, you can add *something* to your daily routine to improve your physical well-being. The truth is, the average person will benefit greatly from something as simple as a brisk 20 to 30-minute walk every day. Doing this, you will find that both your body and your mind become energized. While you walk, focus your thoughts on your vision, your dream, your new business—and the ideas will abound. You will be astonished at the inner brainstorming that takes place. You'll be invigorated, excited, and ready to move your plan forward, returning with solutions to some of your most persistent problems. Staying active physically isn't drudgery or a chore, so don't approach it with that attitude. You've too much to gain to allow negative thoughts to defeat you.

Your attitude: Drop bad habits, develop healthy ones

I'll say this up front: If your bad habit is a substance (drugs or alcohol for example), and you suspect that it has the potential to rise to the level of addiction, then please, seek professional help now. Get yourself back on the road to success and happiness before any more time passes, and before serious damage to your life and your health can occur.

Setting aside ordinary, but distractingly bad habits like sloppiness and dis-organization will help open a direct route to where you're planning to go.

Sloppiness in your appearance (and other areas) can have an effect on what others think of you, and also how you feel about yourself—how *successful* you feel. You may think of it as dressing casual or looking artistic, or that your home has a cozy "lived in" look, but someone else is thinking you don't care *enough*, and thus might not think of you as a candidate for a speaking engagement or consider a fund raiser for your project, and they'll offer it to someone else. You get the idea.

Dressing for success does not always mean dressing *up*. It means dressing for the life part you are planning to play. For example, if it is your dream to be part of an archeological expedition and dig up dinosaur bones, then a tailored business suit is not your best choice of attire. Boots and khakis with roomy pockets would be better.

If disorganization is your downfall, get a handle on it. Start by cleaning your house or apartment. Toss out clutter and give away seldom-used items. If you do this much, you'll start thinking more clearly.

Don't rely on your memory or hastily scribbled notes. Keep a calendar of appointments, including the everyday things you need to get done. Do I have to say it? **Keep your appointments.**

Have I mentioned procrastination? Start with some of the things I just mentioned, like getting rid of clutter in your life. Don't put it off any longer. Return phone calls, do your taxes, fill out application papers that have been sitting on your dining room table. Move forward.

What habits do you need to discard—or develop?

2. **Realigning** personal relationships that are out of sync:

It's difficult to start a new chapter in your life if there is stress or active conflict going on around you. Do what you can to be in harmony with family and friends.

Spend time with your loved ones. Making major changes in your life will require time, dedication, and focus. But don't become so overly focused that you shut your family out of your life, even temporarily.

And if you are in an unhealthy, perhaps even toxic, relationship or friendship that can't be resolved or improved—and it's bringing you down—it may be time to let it go, and move on.

This is also a good time to realign with your spiritual self. It doesn't matter what your spiritual bent, the degree of your eventual success depends upon having balance and contentment in your spiritual life. This is a very personal and subjective thing. It could easily be the subject of another book, but it is in your best interest to find ways that work for you to do this.

3. **Redirecting** your thought patterns:

You can use visualization, meditation, prayer, classes, books, coaching or something else. These all can help shift your thought patterns away from the mistaken idea that it's too late to make changes in your life. Redirect your thoughts back to the possibilities.

Write detailed notes about your re-invented life situation, new business, or the exciting adventure vacation you plan to have. Write about 1) how you'd like it to look, 2) where you will be, 3) what you will be doing, and 4) who you will be with. Keep your notes con-venient so you can look at them from time to time, and add to them if the mood strikes you. Reviewing those notes will reinforce your positive direction and repress any negative thoughts that could become roadblocks.

Create a vision board. Yes, they've been around for a long time, but the truth is, they are powerfully effective when it comes to accomplishing clearly defined objectives. You can use a bulletin

28

board, corkboard, poster board, or your wall. Get some tape, glue, pushpins, even good old thumbtacks, and start pinning.

Speaking of pinning, if you are online regularly, you can use Pinterest.com to make an electronic vision board. It's a free service and easy to use once you get started. At the time of this writing, Pinterest is a young, fast-growing, popular site. Soon other sites could be similar to it, but you get the idea of how you might want to use it as a vision board. Because it involves the use of not just your own, but also other images from various places around the Internet (that may or may not be copyrighted), be sure to familiarize yourself with their terms of service.

The average vision board doesn't have to be fancy, complicated, or involved. Remember, the purpose is to create a clear visual representation of your plan. The images are significant, not the board itself. For example: If you have ever been a salesperson or worked at a company that employed a sales staff, you have seen the star salesperson hard at work on the phone in his/her cubicle. Directly in that star performer's line of sight, is a magazine clipping of a bright, shiny new car (effectively, a single image vision board). I can almost guarantee that six months later, this same salesperson will be driving to work in the car in that picture, exact in every detail, right down to the color. This is how well even a single image vision board works.

My challenge to you: Go deeper than a car, boat or vacation, although these things certainly *can* be part of your vision. Be sure to include relationships, business connections, and the people that will play a significant role in your new chapter.

4. **Rediscovering** the magic in your life:

Focus your thinking on your sense of adventure. Like me, do you remember that feeling and sense of wonder when you were young—and you realized you had your whole life ahead of you? Well, no matter where you are on that timeline, you still do, so embrace it and make use of it.

If you currently don't have a good grasp on that feeling, don't worry. It's still there, deep inside you, probably right where you've been keeping your inner child. She just needs to be coaxed out of hiding and allowed to stretch. Find ways to encourage that, and get yourself to a happier, more relaxed place emotionally. You can, and should do these things for yourself regularly to keep in touch with your inner child. One important reason to resurrect her is because she is not burdened by the weight of your fears and responsibilities. She won't judge you or tell you that you can't follow your dreams.

So go ahead and giggle once in awhile—out loud, just for the fun of it. Run out into your backyard during a summer rain, look up, and feel the warm drops on your face. Make snow angels in winter and mud pies in summer. I'll bet your children or grandchildren will be delighted to help you with any one of these things. They'll love you all the more for it.

Now you've got a start. I'm sure you can come up with several of your own ideas that will take you away from the stresses and worries of the life of a grownup, even if it's just for a few minutes every so often.

5. Removing lingering regrets:

If you have something eating at you, make amends and make up with that person if you can—and get on with your life.

It's true that, over the course of our lives, we're bound to feel regret, shame, or remorse about things we've done or failed to do, the people we've hurt, and the bad choices we've made.

You are not the only person with a past you'd like to reconstruct. Everyone has done things he or she regrets. Unfortunately, none of us gets a do-over in this life. It's futile to torment yourself. Your feelings of regret must be laid aside in order for you to live in the present, and look forward to a better future. Take along only what you learned from those mistakes, and make use of them.

Three simple coping strategies you can use to put your regrets to rest:

a. Express your feelings, cry if you want to, journal about the experience and why it had such a profound effect on your life (or someone else's). If it's a serious issue, then seek professional help or find a support group.

b. Rationalize (I mean this in a positive way). After you express your feelings of regret, think about the incident from a fresh point of view. Foster within yourself a deeper understanding of your actions and avoid judging yourself harshly. You may even be able to see a positive side to it. Then forgive yourself, and accept it as it is.

c. Remind yourself of the many good things you've done in your life. There must be a number of them you can bring to mind. Think especially about something selfless you did for someone, and how it made them feel. Think about the way it made *you* feel. Comfort yourself with the resolution that, in the future, you will be more conscious of your actions and how they affect others, and knowing in your heart that it is unlikely that you will ever again make such a mistake.

To make the trip from ordinary to extraordinary, you must leave your baggage behind.

6. Rewriting your new life chapter:

This is goal setting, pure and simple. My three-tiered approach to goal setting can be adapted to virtually any situation. The length of time you spend at each of these tiers (days, weeks, or months), depends on the nature of the transformation or new chapter you are planning for yourself:

Tier 1. Be realistic with your goals in the beginning in order to acclimate yourself to your new plans. Tier 1 goals should be relatively easy to make happen, but still stretch your capabilities.

- Determine what you need to do— every day—to create your vision.
- Be specific; make an outline and list everything you plan to accomplish.
- Formulate a schedule detailing when and how you'll do each thing.
- Focus and follow through to completion. You will do this again for Tiers 2 and 3.

Right now, as you begin Tier 1, it's important to stress that your commitment to follow through—even with the little things—is critical. I've heard varying statistics, but according to a recent survey taken by Day-Timers, Inc., "...*only one-third of American workers plan their daily schedules. And only 9 percent follow through and complete what they planned.*"

Stick to your original, well-thought-out plan. Yes, you may make minor adjustments along the way, but that's different. If you do this while keeping a clear focus and a strong image of the end result in your mind, you will accomplish your goals.

Tier 2. Raise the bar. At Tier 2, you are ready to raise your expectations and draw out more from yourself—so do it. Divide your vision of the future into workable tasks, and regularly reinforce your vision in your mind and actions, expanding on your previous goal sets.

Reinventing yourself doesn't always go smoothly. You might run into occasional difficulties. But there is one way to keep your compass pointed in the desired direction, even in the face of barriers you may encounter: Don't let your engine stall. Each time you find yourself making excuses as to why

35

you can't do this or go there, ask yourself: What can I do in this moment to keep moving forward? Do *something* to keep your motor running, even if it's a simple thing. Rev that engine.

As you near the end of Tier 2, you might be content having achieved recent goals, thinking, *Wow, I did that. This is great! I can relax now. This is about as far as I imagined I could go, and I'm happy.* Don't stop. You are now ready for the real thing, the brass ring.

Tier 3. Make your final goal a showstopper. It's great to have down-to-earth goals. They are necessary stepping-stones, but at Tier 3, you must open your imagination. Things that seemed out of reach in the past are now within your grasp. This wonderful quote by author and motivational speaker, Bob Proctor, illustrates Tier 3 perfectly:

> ***"Set a goal to achieve something so big, so exhilarating that it excites you and scares you at the same time. It must be a goal so appealing, so much in line with your spiritual core that you can't get it out of your mind."***

This three-tiered goal-setting technique was especially effective for me during my personal transformation (weight-loss) journey and again when I tackled my fear of public speaking. I've mentioned this this before in my other writings.

7. **Revealing** your intentions or **reintroducing** yourself:

In my case, reintroduction was necessary because the changes in my personal appearance due to weight loss were so dramatic that had I not reintroduced myself, most people wouldn't have recognized me. I love telling this story as an example:

One day I was at a restaurant for lunch and ran into a woman I had worked with every day for nearly seven years. I'd not seen her in the last two years (during the time that I was losing weight). I recognized her right away and spoke first, saying, "Hi, what a surprise to see you on this end of town. How have you been?" She looked surprised, but greeted me with a friendly hello. I said some things, and she said some things, but we spoke in generalities. In the back of my mind, I wondered, "Is it possible she doesn't know who I am?" It seemed ridiculous to believe I had changed so much. I didn't want to embarrass her by asking, "Do you know who I am?" or say something silly like, "It's me, Nadia." So we talked—and talked, said our good-byes, and I went back to my table in a bit of a snit because she hadn't even acknowledged my weight loss.

Some minutes later, leaving the restaurant, we saw each other again. This time I was standing with my husband, whom she recognized right away. She came up to me and said, "Nadia, I'm so sorry. I was trying to place you and your voice was familiar, but I didn't recognize you! How much weight *have* you lost?"

Not long after this incident, and one or two others like it, I made a point to get out in public more often and reconnect with old friends and acquaintances. Releasing *Thinking Skinny* also went a long way towards reintroducing myself.

If you're not reintroducing yourself, you can **reveal your intentions** in a number of ways. You can tell someone.

That would be a good start. Better, tell the world: Write an article, start a blog or a Facebook page about your new endeavor, sport, or business.

Mae C. Jemison, the first African-American female astronaut, said these inspiring words:

"Don't let anyone rob you of your imagination, your creativity, or your curiosity...It's your life. Go on and do all you can with it, and make it the life you want to live."

**THREE WOMEN SHARE THEIR STORIES,
AND DESCRIBE HOW THEIR LIVES
MIRROR THE PRINCIPLES IN THIS BOOK**

SID KORPI
AUTHOR, FILM ACTRESS, DANCE INSTRUCTOR, PET CHAPLAIN

Sid Korpi is far too talented and accomplished for me to take credit for anything more than being an inspiration and catalyst for her recent weight loss— something she'd wanted to do for a long time. That's good enough for me. Already athletic, fit, and beautiful, Sid became inspired after reading *Thinking Skinny,* and decided to get healthier still. Losing those extra pounds gave her the edge she needed to pursue a film career with creative Minneapolis filmmaker, Christopher R. Mihm. I recently had a private interview with Sid, and this is how it went:

Nadia: Sid, your life, long before we met, has been a personification of the principles that I teach in this book—and that I live by. I'd like to talk with you about each of the seven steps and hear your unique take on them. We'll start with **#1) Reshaping a healthier body and attitude**. Sid, what was it about my book that resonated with you as you embarked on this new chapter in your life?

Sid: When I learned that I was up for a major role in my first feature film, Chris Mihm's marvelous B&W 1950s-drive-in-style creature feature B-movie, *Attack of the Moon Zombies*, (www.sainteuphoria.com), I knew what wound up 30-feet tall on the silver screen was going to be how I'd be seen forever after. Cameras notoriously add 20 pounds to one's appearance, and given that, though fairly fit, I was already on the high end of "normal" as far as weight charts went. I really wanted to drop those 20 just to come out even.

I'd lived the diet yo-yo my entire life and vowed this was to be the end of that self-destructive cycle. I had your book, *Thinking Skinny*, on my shelf and was drawn to it. I read it in one sitting, let its contents sink in overnight, and awoke the next day ready to lose weight in a sensible, permanent way.

This wasn't a "diet." I know better than to ever tell myself that I "can't" have something; I'm so rebellious, that would simply ensure I'd ruminated on said high-calorie item until I broke down and had too much of it. I planned to lose between one and two pounds per week, and I did just that by still eating whatever I wanted to, just in more reasonable portions. In several months' time, I'd lost roughly 25 pounds, and am approaching two years at this new weight. I knew I could see myself onscreen and not cringe, except for at my scary-looking 1950s bangs, and those were on purpose for the movie.

Nadia: #2) Realigning relationships and spiritual self: To use your own words from a previous interview we had on this subject, you've suffered a tsunami of loss with regard to your family, friends, and relationships. How did you get through it and go on?

Sid: In a few years' time, I lost my mother, stepfather, uncle, three cats, three dogs, a cockatiel, two of my best women friends, and my 15-year marriage. Talk about wiping out everyone you loved, and who you thought loved you. I'll be honest with you; I cried my heart out *every single day* for more than two years. I even had thoughts of suicide during these darkest of days.

As a matter of fact, these thoughts had become so pervasive at one point, I went to the hospital emergency room one Sunday, hoping I could be kept under observation overnight. Instead of receiving any validation or compassion for what I was going through, the ER doctor said, "This isn't a hotel. Go home and call us if you actually have a 'plan' to kill yourself." I was summarily asked to leave the hospital. I had hit my proverbial "rock bottom."

Standing in the doorway of that hospital, more completely alone than I'd ever been in my life, something profound happened that changed me forever. I still remember vividly this sensation I had deep in my chest, at my physical core, of a tiny little flame like that of a candle. I was overwhelmed by a certainty: This core light represented the part of me that belonged to (indeed was one and the same as), the greater Universe. And, it was necessarily just as valuable and worthy of love as all that is eternal.

It came to me in rush that I'd just been presented with an astounding opportunity to learn an invaluable life lesson. I learned that, despite being stripped of every external source of support and compassion, I was still worthwhile. I was still worthy of love.

I joined Emotions Anonymous soon after this event, to rebuild my lost community with people who would understand my struggles, and who would not judge. I never again considered suicide. As I became strong, I was able to help others as I helped myself.

Nadia: #3) Redirecting thought patterns toward the possibilities: I'd love to hear how you do this, Sid. You've had such an eclectic career, and several interesting businesses. Obviously, you are in tune with "possibilities" in a way not found in many other people.

Sid: On a lark, I once visited a psychic at the Renaissance Festival. She told me, almost apologetically, as she read my tarot cards that she saw that I would always be changing from one thing to the next, usually with little to no financial reward, and never settle on one thing as my career. I expect she thought I'd be chagrined about that "news," but instead I said, "Oh, sure, I know that. That's what I love most about myself!"

I am very driven by the need to personally challenge myself. I'll often start some new creative endeavor—like designing jewelry, writing a novel, or singing with an early jazz band—and always see it through to some kind of completion. However, once I win some award or recognition for it, I feel I can move on to the next thing.

I can only stick with things that inherently provide variety, such as my 15 years running, Proof Positive proofreading/freelance writing/wordsmithing business, which never has me composing or reading the same thing twice. Put me in a cubicle, expect me to follow corporate edicts, and make me punch a time clock, and you may as well pronounce me brain-dead on arrival. I've structured my life so it will always be *interesting* for me.

Nadia: #4) Rediscovering the magic in your life: How do you stay young at heart and maintain the fun and excitement in your life?

Sid: I am childfree by choice and have instead opted to retain much that is childlike in me. I feel I'm on a mission to remind adults around me of the importance of playing; of having fun, being creative, joyful, and downright silly; and not giving a fig what others think of them for doing so.

Case in point, I just turned 50 in January, and I threw myself a birthday wake. I rented a coffin, in which I lay as my friends and family "eulogized" me. I'd frequently pop up to laugh at their jokes or throw marshmallows at anyone who got too into "roasting" me. We held this in a church basement and had a reception of Jell-O salads and tater tot hot dish among the delicious items in the Church Basement Ladies potluck buffet. I try to be a role model for authentic eccentricity.

Nadia: #5) Removing lingering regrets: Each of us must find ways to do this. How have you managed?

Sid: Most of us are more likely to be kinder to strangers than we are to ourselves. To correct that inequity, start by admitting your mistakes without blaming others in any way for your actions, even if they're deeply involved.

You're no one's victim as long as you learn and grow from any experience. Forgive yourself for things you were too afraid to do, for opportunities you missed, and take baby steps toward finding and freeing your inner courage—and reward those steps. Forgive yourself for wishing and hoping you could change someone else in order to attain the love and acceptance you could/should have been giving yourself all along. Forgive yourself for accepting responsibility for things that really were beyond your control. The fact is you've screwed up in the past; you'll no doubt screw up again in the future. Just try not to keep screwing up in the exact same ways over and over. That's nuts.

Nadia: #6) Rewrite a new life chapter:
When I first heard you tell the story of how you set your sights on appearing in a Christopher Mihm film, and how you went about that, it was obvious to me that you set a goal, focused on it and followed through to completion. Please tell it here.

Sid: I had read about this local filmmaker who was dedicated to making black-and-white, 1950s-style horror movies. My new husband and I attended the world premiere of his third movie, *Cave Women on Mars*. I determined then and there that before I died, I had to have something to do with one of this guy's movies. So I decided to stalk him.

Actually, all that entailed was one email, but "stalking" sounds more melodramatic. In my email, I mentioned that I was willing to be an extra, a prop mistress, a dead body, whatever he needed. I downloaded a photo of my high school theater trophy that named me Outstanding Dramatic Performer of 1980, with the caption, "Proof I'm talented."

I'd also read that he liked to write his movie scripts with places in mind where he knew he could shoot, rather than have to build sets or scout locations. So, I offered him the use of our third-floor dance studio, which is decorated like a '50s malt shop, and invited him to visit it sometime. A month or so passed before he finally responded, but he took me up on my offer to check out the room.

Two movies later, my husband and I were given walk-on roles in *Destination: Outer Space* with one line apiece—actually the exact same line. We each got to say, "Greetings, Wise One."

I helped out as "script Nazi" after our scene was shot (i.e., reading the robot's part and making sure leading man Josh Craig remembered all his lines). Perhaps it was then that Chris noticed I could actually speak more than three words in succession of his purposely clunky dialogue and tucked away that knowledge for future reference because he gave me a leading role in his next movie, *Attack of the Moon Zombies.*

Anyway, long story short, the movie rocked the world, I won a Best Actress in a Zombie Movie Dead Letter award from MailOrderZombie.com, and I was subsequently cast as Leigh, the eccentric dog lady/haunted-home owner, in Mihm's 2012 film, *House of Ghosts.* This movie was actually filmed in our house though, ironically, not in the third-floor malt shop. That's going to be featured in an upcoming giant-spider movie.

Nadia: #7) Reveal and live your intentions: Please bring me up to date on new things in your life now, and on the horizon.

Sid: A few years back, I made a deal with myself that I wouldn't audition for any plays anymore. Mostly it was because of the time commitment, and I would only do them if they fell into my lap—so I'd know they were meant to be. That philosophy got me the roles of Gertrude in Steve Martin's comic play *The Underpants,* Mrs. Ellie Banks in *Father of the Bride,* and Jeri Neal in *The Dixie Swim Club.*

Since making these Mihm movies, I've been in two short independent films with burgeoning filmmakers Timothy Printup and Katie Cragoe, *Treasure Box* and *Breaking for Home*.

My costar in *House of Ghosts*, Justen Overlander (Ray), a hilarious writer/actor/director himself, offered me the role of Goldie in his new movie, *The Bequeather*. It's a comedy along the lines of *Young Frankenstein* set in the 1950s—my favorite era. Filming began in May 2012. And as I mentioned earlier, Chris Mihm is working on a giant spider movie, as part of a drive-in double feature. I know I'm to be in it in some capacity, but I don't know exactly what my role will be yet.

Nadia: I can appreciate your willingness to risk failure. You "get it," and the potential rewards are unbelievable if you can let go of this fear. What advice do you have for others who seek to follow their passions as you have yours?

Sid: I've often joked that I've failed at more things than most people do in a dozen lifetimes. But the word in need of redefining there is "failed." I've only failed at anything if its success is measured in dollar signs, brand new sports cars, and vacation homes in the Bahamas. For me, success is measured by how many of my various talents I've been able to explore in unique ways, regardless of the fiscal payoff, and how much my creativity has added to the value of my life and the lives of those around me.

For instance, the book I was spiritually guided to write after my tsunami of loss, *Good Grief: Finding Peace After Pet Loss,* has won four literary awards—including "Best Self-Help Book of the Year" from Premier Book Awards—and I continually hear from people about how much it has helped them navigate their grief after losing a beloved animal companion. Is it a *New York Times* Bestseller? Nope. But its topic has staying power; it continues to sell at a fairly steady pace, and is even coming due for a second edition printing. I risked a lot of my own money to get it published, and I have earned back every penny and am now actually a little in the black. Writing it has led to my getting public speaking gigs, too, which represents another modest revenue stream.

Lest you think I lie around eating bonbons all day, however, I'll have you know I also operate several other home-based businesses: Proof Positive Editing, my bread-and-butter business for the past 20 years; Noncon-formist Nuptials, wherein I write and officiate wedding ceremonies for those who balk at the traditional, cookie-cutter approach; and Two Right Feet Dance, through which my husband and I teach beginning social dances like swing, rumba, waltz, etc. Our motto is

"Forget Fred and Ginger—we'll have you dancing like Fred and Wilma in no time!"

I've weathered this great recession better than most because, frankly, I'm used to being broke. Subsequently, I had less to lose both financially and emotionally in the economic downturn. I believe I can adapt to change a bit more easily than most because I've always had to diversify or die. But each of these endeavors represents a different colorful thread in the gorgeous tapestry of my life. I don't do beige. Instead, I say, "Bring on the rainbow hues!"

Sid Korpi, the human caregiver to seven rescued pets, is a compulsively creative person and is known to act in B-movies for food. She is grateful to be married to an understanding man who thinks life with her and all the critters is an adventure. Her websites are:
> *www.goodgriefpetloss.com*
> *www.tworightfeetdance.com*
> *www.nonconformistnuptials.com.*

KATHRYN MAYLEEN HOLMES OVERCAME PARALYSIS AND BEGAN LIVING A BRIGHT NEW CHAPTER IN HER LIFE

Kathi Holmes' resilient spirit gave her the courage to conquer challenges few of us ever endure. She came out on the other side of the rainbow with renewed faith and a surprising new chapter in her life as an author. I had the pleasure of hearing Kathi's story in person. This is what she shared with me about her ordeal:

Nadia: Kathi, You've been through something few people will ever have to face. You suffered damage to your spinal cord and were told you would never walk again. How did you change your situation as it relates to the seven principles we're talking about in this book?

As regards **step #1) Reshaping a healthier body and attitude**, Kathi, what do you think were the catalysts that gave you the mental and emotional strength to believe you could walk again?

Kathi: When I was told I would never walk again, I prepared myself with everything I needed to be able to function the best I could with my disability. While in the rehab center, even though I really believed I would not walk, I went about my therapy with all the energy and stamina I could muster. I am from a family of strong women with a firm work ethic. I was determined to do my best. Every small accomplishment pushed me to try a little harder. When I could stand for just one minute, I was encouraged to try for one minute 15 seconds, then 30. Each accomplishment pushed me further. My experience was similar to that described in the song, *High Hopes,* about the ant and the rubber tree plant.

Nadia: #2) Realigning relationships and spiritual self: Your husband was going through a devastating illness simultaneously to yours, leaving you essentially alone in your journey. How did you cope?

Kathi: Although my husband, Charlie, was not physically with me, he was always available on the other end of the telephone. We used to call each other and compare lunches to see who had the tastiest meal. We were apart but not alone. Although I had always depended on Charlie's feedback when making big decisions, I was now often forced to make quick decisions on my own. When the doctors asked me whether I wanted to risk my life having surgery on my spine, I consulted Charlie, my daughter, and my son.

It was a unanimous decision to decline. The doctors felt this was a good decision, given my health history. Each person responds to crisis differently. Charlie is a calm, analytical person with sound judgment. My daughter needs facts laid out before her. She was instrumental in getting the doctors to fully explain my condition. My daughter was with me at my worst. I could feel her deep concern. When she left the room, I asked her boyfriend (now husband) if he would stay with her while I was going through all this. He said he would be there for her forever. I felt relieved. Like Charlie and me, my son too is calm, but also the one who checked in every day to see how I was doing. In Charlie's absence, both my children were there for me. We have a small but very close family. And God. I felt He was always with me. Yet I could not pray for my recovery. Others did. I could not. All I asked is that He give me the strength to accept the challenges ahead. My only prayer was, "Thy will be done."

Nadia: #3) Redirecting thought patterns toward the possibilities: Please tell us more about what was going on in your head and how you suppressed negative thoughts and feelings of hopelessness?

Kathi: When I was first paralyzed, I could not even roll over in bed by myself. I felt helpless and vulnerable. I didn't want to be a burden on my husband or my children. There was a brief time when I thought, "What good am I now?" I quickly snapped out of that and realized I was left with all my upper body strength, my eyes, my ears, and my brain. I could still be productive. I just needed to look at life differently than I had in the past. My vision was *focused forward*; on what I could accomplish, not what I had lost.

Nadia: #4) Rediscovering the magic in your life: After months of exhausting physical therapy, you gradually responded, to the surprise of your doctors and even yourself. Once you were making progress, how did you find ways to bring joy back into your life?

Kathi: Joy came the day I arrived home, and my daughter had prepared my new room with fresh flowers and sunshine-yellow drapes and bedspread. Joy came the day I entered the Courage Center pool for rehabilitation. I have always loved the water, and I felt more "normal," even though I needed weights to keep my legs below me, which meant I never knew where my feet were positioned. I could hardly contain myself the day Charlie and I, along with my aide, took the Metro Mobility bus to my daughter's wedding. I even danced at her wedding (with my friend on my lap as I wheeled my power chair around the floor). I had joy on Christmas Eve 2009 when my son assisted me to his car, and we drove through a blinding snowstorm to reach the hospital where my daughter was having my first grandchild. Joy is all around us. All we need to do is see it and enjoy it. The first time I drove my power chair through the wooded area near our home, I heard every leaf rustling, every bird singing, and even talked to a squirrel. When you lose something, there is overwhelming joy in finding it again.

Nadia: #5) Removing lingering regrets: Were there regrets that you needed to deal with or put into perspective during this ordeal?

Kathi: If I say I wish I had never been paralyzed, I would have missed many lessons of life that I learned. I would never have exercised my patience. I would never have been as compassionate toward people with disabilities. I would never have had my faith strengthened. As I came out of my paralysis, the sun began to shine brighter and brighter each day. How can I have regrets?

Nadia: #6) Rewrite a new life chapter: How did you come to write this book?

Kathi: I always thought it would be fun to write a book. When many people expressed interest in how I was able to heal, I realized I needed to share my experience to give hope to others with life challenges. I have always encouraged everyone I meet to realize their passion. The book has given me an opportunity to reach out to others—to spread a message of hope. I could not have realized a better dream for myself.

Nadia: #7) Reveal and live your intentions: Now that you are published, you are making public appearances, having book signings, and speaking. Please talk about that.

Kathi: The best part of reaching out to others is the feedback I receive. Not just what the book meant to them or how it encouraged them to move beyond their current boundaries, but their success stories. Courage doesn't always make the front page of the newspaper. It's with us every day, if we only listen.

Nadia: What advice do you have for others who seek to follow their passions as you have yours?

Kathi: None of us knows what the future has in store for us. All we can do is live life doing the best we can with what we have. Through courage, determination, and faith, you can have hope.

Kathryn M. Holmes' career encompasses the area of counseling, advertising, marketing, and publishing. She has written for both business and pleasure. Working full-time and raising a family, Kathi spent nearly 15 years diligently completing her college education, one class at a time. She began with a focus on counseling, conducting several support groups, later switching to a communications major. She and her husband Charlie, live in Minnetonka, Minnesota. She can be reached at k.m.holmes@comcast.net or www.IStandWithCourage.com.

BARB GREENBERG, AUTHOR, SPEAKER, BUSINESS WOMAN

Barb Greenberg suddenly found herself divorced and alone after 33 years of marriage. She worked through her pain, found healing and wholeness, and eventually found a way to share what she had learned with other women in similar situations.

Barb and I talked recently about how she rebuilt her life, and how some the things she did paralleled the seven steps in this book:

Nadia: Barb, like a lot of women, your divorce came after many years of marriage. The shock of such a shift must have rocked your well-being, emotionally as well as physically.

Can you tell us how you held up and some of the things you did to stay well as it relates to what we're talking about in step **#1) Reshaping a healthier body and/or attitude**?

Barb: My divorce, and the years leading up to it, were such a difficult and painful time in my life. In 1998, my college-age daughter was in a life-threatening car accident halfway around the world, in Australia. Her recovery was a miracle, and watching her fight to regain her life gave me the courage to do the same. Three years later, after much soul-searching, I filed for divorce after 33 years of marriage.

Struggling to reclaim my life and stay healthy during this crisis, taught me to become much better at listening to my body. When I needed to move, I moved. When I needed to be still, I rested.

I also began to listen to the whispers of my heart, and to trust what I knew to be true. I had silenced and ignored that voice for so many years, and now the more I listened, the stronger it became.

During this time, I decided to travel light. Leaving the home I had shared with my husband for over 20 years, I took only those things I really cherished, trusting I was making room for new treasure to come into my life.

Nadia: #2) Realigning relationships and spiritual self: For the first time since you were young, you were alone, and your life had been turned upside down. How did you realign other relationships in your life, and what about your spiritual well-being?

Barb: As my relationship with myself improved, so did my relationship with my family, especially with my adult daughters. As for friends, during a divorce you are never quite sure who is going to get custody of them. Relationships with my true friends deepened. And those who drifted away cleared a space for new friends to arrive, bringing such beautiful light into my life.

My sense of spirituality also deepened. I say "thank you" more often and about more things. I believe more deeply that life is unfolding in my highest good. And I do my best to be more attuned to the energy of the divine in everyday life.

Nadia: #3) Redirecting thought patterns toward the possibilities: What was going on in your thoughts as you rebuilt your life? How did you keep negative thoughts at bay and maintain a positive outlook?

Barb: Surrounding myself with wonderful friends, and doing what I love, has always been the best way for me to maintain a positive outlook.

As for keeping negative thoughts at bay, I learned something very interesting during my divorce. One night I was so frightened, I couldn't fall asleep. Every time I closed my eyes, my mind swirled. "What was going to happen to me? How was I going to survive? How could I ease my children's pain?"

I turned on the bedroom light, grabbed a pen and a legal pad, and began writing "I'm scared. I'm scared, I'm so, so scared." I wrote this over and over, using the entire legal pad, sometimes pressing the pen so hard I ripped through the paper. The result, surprisingly, was that I calmed down, and had the best night's sleep I'd had in a months.

For me, there was tremendous value in acknowledging my negative thoughts, and letting them have their say. Once they had been heard, they returned much less frequently and with much less intensity.

When it came to rebuilding my life and my business, I did my best to follow those whispers from my heart. My vision board became a drawing of a daisy. In the center of the flower is the phrase "Sharing Stories That Heal." A word on one petal is "Speaking," a word on another is "Writing," and on another is "Divorce Support," and so on. Some petals have nothing written on them yet because I am always open to new ways to blossom. It's a bit corny, but I love it.

Nadia: #4) Rediscovering the magic in your life: At what point did you know everything would eventually be okay, perhaps even better than before?

Barb: As soon as I made the decision to divorce, even though I was terrified and overwhelmed, I felt somewhere deep inside of me that things would be better.

I do know exactly when I *consciously* realized life was improving. I had moved out of our house and into a small, cozy apartment. Many days I would come home, toss my keys on the table and sigh, "I'm 53 years old, and I'm all alone in this little apartment." Then one day, I woke up early, sat up, stretched out my arms and proclaimed happily, "I'm 53 years old, and I'm all alone in this little apartment!"

Nadia: #5) Removing lingering regrets: Were there regrets you needed to deal with or put into perspective during this time period?

Barb: Oh, yes, so many. At the top of my list were:

- Why didn't I leave sooner?
- Why didn't I see what was happening in my life?
- Why didn't I protect my children better?
- How could I have been so blind to what was happening?

It took a long time to forgive myself and to understand I was doing the best I could, just like everyone else. Journaling helped me sort things out. Good friends helped remind me I had value. Walking in nature helped. And sitting with my cat on my lap worked miracles. We all come to points in our lives when it is just too much work to continue to carry so much regret. When that happens, we are ready to set down our burden and move forward with the joy of new possibilities.

Nadia: #6) Rewrite a new life chapter: You were inspired to write a book that is now helping other women going through divorce. How did that process come about?

Barb: I began my first book, *Hope Grew Round Me*, in 1998, after a dear friend suggested I write the story of how my daughter's life-threatening accident and recovery planted the seeds for my own self-discovery. What a surprise to be in my fifties, discover how much I love to write, and have a new world open up.

When I became very skeptical about the "happily ever after" endings of fairy tales, I wrote my second book. *After the Ball: A Woman's Tale of Reclaiming Happily Ever After.* It is a lovely fairy tale that follows what happens to Cinderella and Snow White— later! And their journey resonates with women who are single, married, divorced, or remarried because it reminds each of us we have the power to transform our lives.

When I write, my goal setting is not structured or formal. I never lose sight of my dream and of the responsibility I feel to move a story into the world so it can make a difference for someone else. I do my best to be consistent, and I can be quite stubborn when I need to.

Nadia: #7) Reveal and live your intentions: Now that you are published, you are making public appearances and speaking to women's groups. What has this been like? What has the response been from your audience?

Barb: Public speaking has been a complete joy and a complete surprise to me, especially, since like you, Nadia, I was so very shy growing up. Recognizing the power that comes when women connect with each other, I created a monthly **After the Ball** program, offering divorce support for women. When I share my story, others tell me they feel less alone. They feel uplifted, inspired, and understand they can become the heroines of their own story.

Nadia: Do you have any advice to share?

Barb: I believe that when women heal, families heal. When families heal, communities heal. And when communities heal, the possibilities are endless. I am so grateful that I have taken the chance to *create a new chapter in my life.*

Barb Greenberg is the author of "Hope Grew Round Me" *and* "After the Ball: a Woman's Tale of Reclaiming Happily Ever After" *she lives in Minnesota and is actively mentoring other women going through divorce. Her website is www.BarbGreenberg.com.*

TWO INSPIRING PEOPLE

A Special Thank You

In closing, I'd like to tell you about the two people who have inspired me the most in my life. I'm certain they can also inspire you. To tell their story, I'll need to go all the way back to 1979.

Norman and Sylvia Wilkins, at the age of 50, after raising four children to adulthood, sold their dairy farm in Motley, Minnesota, loaded up a 1964 Freightliner semi-tractor and trailer with 73,000 pounds of gear and equipment, said good-bye to family and friends, and set out to carve a new life for themselves on the frozen tundra of Alaska.

They built a log cabin and lived there for 27 years, living off the land and what little income they had. For the first several years,

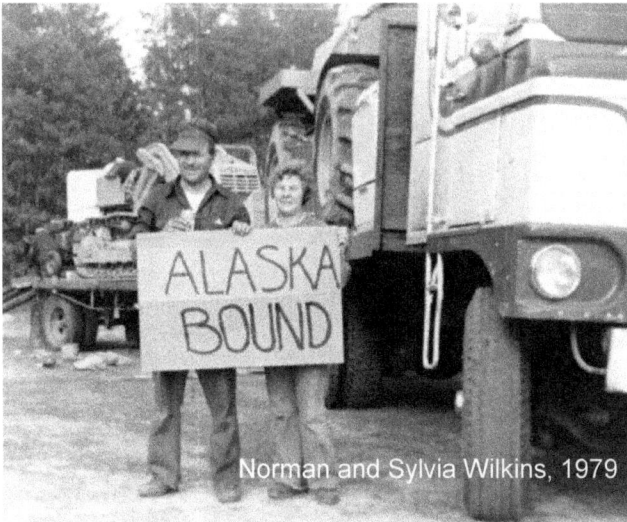

Norman and Sylvia Wilkins, 1979

they had no electricity, running water, or indoor plumbing. Norman trapped for furs, hunted their food, and prospected for gold. Sylvia, still missing her children and grandchildren in the lower 48, made new friends and built a large garden in a forbidding and very short growing climate. Much of what she grew had to be started indoors with the help of a greenhouse they built. She sewed and repaired clothing, both by hand and with a treadle machine; picked berries and made preserves; and cleaned and canned salmon. Together, they dressed out, packaged and prepared moose, bear, caribou, and other game.

All through those years, Norman chronicled their adventures in his daily journal entries. Recently, I transcribed those journals for Norman and compiled and published them as a three-volume documentary journal, *10,000 Days in Alaska* by Norman Wilkins. Site: www.10000daysinalaska.com.

Why do I know so much about these people? They are my parents, and I can't be more proud than I am today to claim them. I never tire of hearing them tell their stories, and I've never lost my sense of amazement at what they have done. At this writing (2012), they are in their mid-80s and have reluctantly left Alaska and moved back to Minnesota due to health issues.

I'm making an effort to be as unique and full of adventure as they are. I expect that means I'll have some surprises yet ahead of me. I wonder what they will be?

IN CONCLUSION

Now, it's time for *you* to do the things you always said you were going to do or replace outdated dreams with better ones—and follow through. I'm not talking about a bucket list to mark off items one by one saying, "There, I did that." I'm talking about *living*.

Not only is it okay for you to dream, it's a necessary part of this entire process. Your dreams are more real than you imagine, and they are the first steps toward creating new chapters in your life.

This is not new thinking. A long time ago, Henry David Thoreau put it this way:

"If you have built castles in the air,
your work need not be lost;
that is where they should be.
Now put the foundations under them."

Think of your best life as a book
with you as the author,
and ask yourself what chapters
are yet to be written.
–Nadia Giordana

ABOUT THE AUTHOR

Nadia Giordana hosts an Internet and public access TV show titled Woman*Vision TV* and is the author of the award-winning book, *Thinking Skinny*.

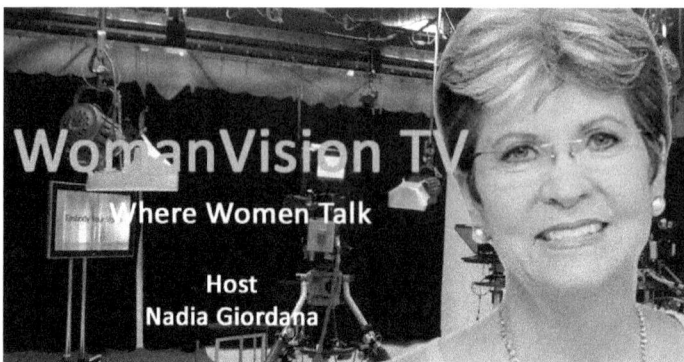

Nadia was born to a mother who during WWII, became a displaced person, a woman without a country. Much of her early life was not of her own design. From her, Nadia learned great patience and a strong desire to live life with purpose and intent.

From her father, a farmer turned trapper, hunter, and gold prospector, she inherited a practical, *do-it-now-rather-than-later* work ethic. From him she also acquired a sense of wonder and adventure electrified by the knowledge that the world we live in has more to offer than most can imagine. We need only to let go of the familiar and make a leap of faith to land in an exciting new environment.

Author's websites and social media access:

EmbodyYourVision.com
ThinkingSkinny.com
WomanVision.tv
NadiaGiordana.com
Twitter: @NadiaGiordana
linkedin.com/in/nadiagiordana

Facebook.com/nadia.giordana.media

NOTES

Use the following pages to write down your preliminary goals.

www.ingramcontent.com/pod-product-compliance
Lightning Source LLC
LaVergne TN
LVHW051755080426
835511LV00018B/3325